P9-BYO-580

Children and Grief:
Big Issues for Little Hearts

Johnette Hartnett

Copyright © 1993 by Johnette Hartnett
Edited/Designed by Ellen Hogan

All rights reserved, including the right to reproduce this book or
portions thereof in any form, by any means, electronic or
mechanical, including photo-copying and recording, or by any
storage or retrieval system, excepting brief quotes used in
connection with reviews, without the permission in writing from
the publisher.

Published by Good Mourning, P.O. 9355, South Burlington, VT
05407-9355; distributed by same.

ISBN: 1-883171-87-3 (Volume 5)
ISBN: 1-883171-81-4 (6 Volume Set)
Library of Congress Catalog Card Number: 93-90778

The Good Mourning Series has been partially funded by a
grant from the National Funeral Directors Association (NFDA).

This book is dedicated to my three cherubs,
as I so often called them.

DAVID JOHN
July 4, 1971 - March 8, 1983

JOHNETTE THERESE
December 19, 1972 - March 8, 1983

JOHN PETER
May 28, 1974 - March 8, 1983

All your past except its beauty is gone,
and nothing is left but a blessing.
                                        – A Course in Miracles

Children and Grief:
Big Issues for Little Hearts

Contents

Foreword

On March 8, 1983, my three children and housekeeper died in a fire in St. Albans, Vermont. My son David John was eleven years old; my daughter, Johnette Therese, was nine; and my son John Peter was eight. Our housekeeper, Nancy, was twenty-one.

Until that day I was a busy and happy woman. Although I was facing a divorce, my life was full with children, a busy professional career and rewarding community work.

Until that day, I belonged to an elite and extremely fortunate group of people to whom such tragedies simply did not happen. We lived in an idyllic small New England town, conspicuously and deliberately lacking the traffic, crime and social ills that plague big cities. We watched those things happen to other people in the movies and on TV or in the newspapers. In our insulated, tight-knit community, we were protected. We were financially secure and the children were healthy, intelligent, talented and athletic. Nothing could happen to us.

Then in the spark of a smoldering ember, our defenses failed, the plan to keep us safe from unspeakable horror disintegrated, and the unimaginable became a reality.

Not one, but all three of my children died. Together. Of smoke inhalation.

The effects, I probably do not need to tell you, have been excruciating, deep and lasting. During the first five years following the fire, I spent many, many hours in therapy sorting out the sometimes sordid events that led to and followed the tragedy. My therapy included sessions with three different professionals whose unique perspectives offered valuable guidance and counsel at different stages of my grief.

In addition to seeking professional help, I amassed a personal arsenal to guard against the waves of pain that to this day rise and subside in a sometimes destructive, sometimes therapeutic sea of sadness.

I have aggressively sought out detailed information on grief and the painful aftermath of death. In the past ten years, I have collected a library of research and attended countless seminars, workshops and professional-level courses. I've spent long hours among practitioners in the fields of mental health, grief, funeral and health-care. Through widening ripples of friendships and business associates, I have met, counseled and learned from others who have lost loved ones and who are searching for the same solace I seek.

Freud said that grief is a natural response to loss. I believe that Freud and his modern successors do not go far enough. For many people who have never experienced a loss, this "natural response" certainly seems like anything *but* natural or normal when it happens to you.

Cultural changes that have taken place over the last fifty to one hundred years have made grief all the more unnatural: Strong religious and community ties, close family units, well-preserved ceremonies and traditions used to lend unfailing support to bereaved families and friends. So many of those traditions have fallen by the wayside. As a culture we have handed over the care of our dying, our aged and our dead to institutions. A century ago, eighty percent of Americans died at home; today, eighty percent die in institutions. We are ignoring death until it hits us squarely in the face. Even then, we are trying to pretend it doesn't happen: Many cremations and burials take place without a funeral or memorial service of any kind.

At the same time, funeral directors are reporting a revealing and rather sad trend: Because funeral professionals are the only association many bereaved people have with death, grieving family members are drifting back to funeral homes for grief support, months after the deaths of their loved ones.

Not only do we lack knowledge of what to do, how to act or how to resolve grief issues for ourselves, we are also adrift and uncomfortable when faced with friends and acquaintances who are grieving. Amazingly, while I struggled with my grief, friends slowly dropped out of my life. The overprotective remark I always got when I asked, "Why? Why doesn't So-and-So call?" was, "You must understand, Johnette, people just don't know what to do or say." I would wonder how these people thought *I* would handle losing my whole family. I had never lost a whole family before. I didn't understand how to do it. I often found myself comforting *others* because of my loss. I became the expert on how to survive tragedy. In order to survive I had to teach others about loss.

Finally, like many people valiantly paddling in the wake of tragedy and grief, I have come to believe that perhaps the only way to make sense of the chaos is to help others. While many people are blessed with an innate ability to communicate compassion and strength and perspective in the presence of the bereaved, many more people are not so blessed.

I have seen a dire need to help people identify, understand and prepare for the process of grief.

Children and Grief: Big Issues for Little Hearts is the fifth in a series of six books I have written to address some of the most common issues I've come across in my recovery and in my research.

The entire series includes:

1. *Using Grief to Grow: A Primer*
   How You Can Help/How to Get Help

2. *Different Losses Different Issues:*
   What to Expect and How to Help.

3. *The Funeral: An Endangered Tradition*
   Making Sense of the Final Farewell

4. *Grief in the Workplace:*
   40 Hours Plus Overtime

5. *Children and Grief:*
   Big Issues for Little Hearts

6. *Death Etiquette for the '90s:*
   What to Do/What to Say

These books are written in an easy-to-pick-up, browse and digest, question-and-answer format. I have attempted to be complete without being overwhelming.

Some issues are supplemented with supporting anecdotes, separated from the rest of the text by this symbol: ☙ .

In addition, I refer throughout the text to my other books, which may expand on questions of particular interest to you.

Please accept my sincere hope that you and the bereaved person you are concerned about will benefit from these practical, sensible books.

Johnette Hartnett
Burlington, VT 1993

Introduction

Timmy, age 12, at summer camp with friends:

"Oh, my father? He's a salesman. He's always on the road. That's why he doesn't ever bring me to camp."

(Timmy's father had been dead for three years.)

Jane, age 9:

"I know if I had only got along better with my brothers, Mom wouldn't have died. She always told me I would be the death of her."

Mary, age 4:

"I know Grandpa died, but when will he come for dinner, again?"

Children and death. There probably isn't a less favorite topic. But, whether we like it or not, children experience and grieve over losses everyday. Like adults, they need time to heal and to integrate losses into their lives. How well they learn to work through their grief depends on the same variables (social, physical, cultural, religious, environmental, etc.) that apply to adults, but with one main catch. Most children grieve according to the developmental and cognitive stages they are in at the time of their losses.

So a four-year-old might listen attentively as you explain the death of her grandfather only to ask later on when she will see her grandfather again. The notion that death is reversible is normal and natural for her age.

Many adults have learned to tell fact from fantasy, verbalize feelings and communicate fears. But even with all these "developed" abilities and acquired knowledge, many bereaved adults find the road to recovery rough and difficult. Imagine that same road for a child who cannot read or speak or has yet to learn to conceptualize his own feelings of anxiety and loss! How do these children cope with the death of a loved one?

Children who experience the death of a close loved one grow up with their "losses." Birthdays, holidays, graduations, and marriages are monumental reminders for children who have lost a parent or sibling. Many adults are still grieving the loss of a parent or sibling from their childhood. Sometimes the effects of these childhood losses are not recognized until the adult is challenged with yet another loss in adulthood. Some adults go through their entire lives never recognizing that the underlying sadness and emptiness they daily experience is part of some unfinished grief.

Traditionally, children are the least recognized group of grievers. Bereaved children are often passed off as being "too young to realize what's happening." Today experts and research tell us this just isn't so. Some experts say children grieve as early as six months and that death deeply affects their psychological, emotional, and sometimes even their physiological development.

When we look at the topic of children and death, we cannot help but view the important role parents and teachers play. Many parents, when faced with the death of a spouse or child, are not aware of the effect the death will have on surviving children. The fact is that surviving children will grieve in spite of all their developmental limitations. The death of "others" (neighbors, relatives, classmates) may adversely effect a child in many ways. A recent study linked delinquency in adolescents to the death of a close family member. Another study found a higher incidence of depression in women who lose a mother before the age of ten.

Children don't "get over" deaths – they have to work through them just as adults do. We know a death acts as an interruption and interferes with the normal stages of development and growth in children. Children will benefit as parents and educators become knowledgeable about the effects of grief on children.

Today, many children are learning to cope with life adversities in all too "adult" ways, and alarmingly they are acquiring these coping skills at earlier and earlier ages. The fact that thousands of children today are using suicide, alcohol, and drugs to solve life issues is astounding, but not so unexpected when we look at present-day history.

Children are raised in a culture that encourages prolonging life at any cost, yet they see that same culture spend billions on "star wars." They are taught that it is perfectly acceptable to hire out the care of the aged, the terminally ill and the dead. Many are taught that "old" is worthless. Young people today are exposed constantly to impersonal death, while the experience with "real death" of someone they know or love has become increasingly rare. When children are bereaved they are often shocked and overwhelmed and unprepared for the experience.

We have not been a model society for teaching children how to deal with death and aging because we are not very good at it ourselves. Our urban lifestyle has increased the depersonalization of our overall quality of community life. A disturbing side effect is a generation poorly equipped to deal with the death and dying experience and whose rate of teenage suicide has become the second leading cause of death after accidents.

It is estimated that children have viewed "tens of thousands" of deaths on television by the time they are old enough to vote. Violence and death are intimate parts of children's lives today. The frequency of the violence/death theme in literature, newsprint, TV, films, music, and toys is a major factor in promoting the impersonal, death-denying attitude so prevalent in our country. Children are developing a fascination about violence and horror by exposure to mutilations and special-effects gore.

When we look at the present-day death-denying environment our children live in we get a glimpse of a rather serious dilemma. How can a society respond to or acknowledge the needs of bereaved children when in fact they are not aware of those needs themselves? How can children express grief when in fact their natural reactions are conditioned (or desensitized) daily by overexposure to death and violence? How can we teach children that the feelings they experience when someone they love dies are normal and okay if we don't understand those feelings ourselves? How can children develop healthy attitudes about death when it is often portrayed to them as glamorous and as an antidote to many life problems? How can children learn a healthy and meaningful response to loss when their own death traditions and rituals are being challenged, if not eliminated, by our present death-denying society? How do we teach children not to fear death if we fear it ourselves?

This book explores the factors that may hinder or help children at all stages of development in dealing with the loss of a loved one. It offers practical and helpful suggestions for adults in assisting children to acknowledge and process their grief.

How Age May Affect
Grief in Children

Infants, Toddlers and Pre-schoolers
(Birth to Two Years)

Experts say children as young as six months experience the anxiety of separation. One of the first games played with infants is the familiar "peek-a-boo" game. This expression actually came from the Old English, meaning "dead or alive." Infants enjoy experimenting and testing the idea that Mommy or Daddy can disappear for a few seconds and then reappear.

It is during the first two years of life that children learn to trust their environment. Many of the early, exasperating, repetitive games toddlers enjoy (like drop all the toys and let Mommy pick them up), teach object identification and develop important motor skills.

The death of a parent in the first two years of a child's life often interferes with the normal development of trust between the remaining parent, the child, and his environment. All of a sudden the child's primary care giver is no longer around. Who will meet his needs? In addition, the child usually has not developed verbal skills, so communicating feelings is extremely difficult.

Many children who lose a parent at this stage become withdrawn, show loss of appetite, and exhibit crankiness. Their symptoms may be strikingly similar to adult grief reactions. Children in this stage who are bereaved should be surrounded with familiar faces and treated with consistency.

Pre-schoolers *(Two to Five)*

Just a few of the developmental issues the child is addressing in this stage are toilet training, learning to associate objects with words, developing vocabulary, exploring independence, learning about personal and environmental limits, developing initiative, and seeking approval.

In this stage the child has begun to use language to build his conceptual foundation. This will help him understand and communicate his experiences with separation and loss.

During the early part of this stage, children think of death as reversible. Much of their experience with death on TV confirms this temporary death concept. Because they have not developed their logical thinking skills yet, it is normal for them to think of death as a "place" that you go to, but then return from. Adults often encourage this concept by using phrases like "gone to sleep," "gone to heaven," "on a trip" when discussing the death of a loved one with a child. A child at this age may ask how someone can go to the bathroom, celebrate birthdays and holidays, or breathe when he is buried in the ground.

Children are often interested in what happens to the body and body parts when there has been a death. At this stage they become concerned about their own body and are concerned about body mutilation. It is normal for children to ask questions about the dead body, although that may sound indelicate or inappropriate to an adult.

During the latter part of this stage, as children begin to develop their social and behavioral skills, they begin to learn about guilt. If a five-year-old wishes his three-year-old sister dead because she keeps interrupting his play and she dies the next day, the older child may feel responsible. He actually thinks his thoughts caused the death. Adults should do a little investigative work to make sure that a bereaved child doesn't harbor such guilt. We call this "magical thinking" in children, but many adults use this same type of thinking when they are bereaved.

The death of a pet is an opportune time to introduce children to the concept of death. A funeral for the pet acquaints them with ritual and tradition, as simple as it may be.

Childhood Years *(Six to Eleven)*

The experts tell us children in this range are most concerned about achievement and failure. It is a time when they begin to use logic to solve problems, although they are yet to become adept at abstract thinking. Children begin to understand the concept that death is permanent. They are self-centered during this stage and develop magical reasons for why a lot of things happen. Death is not excluded. Children in this age group often think of death as someone (a ghost, the Grim Reaper, a monster, the bad guy) and they don't really believe death can happen to them personally.

Often when a sibling dies, a child in this stage will fear for his own life. Will this happen to me? Will my body stop? Their skills of logic are still developing, so explanations about a death and what happens after death need to be very clear. Explanations of what is done with the body, cremation or burial, need to be explained in simple but clear terms.

Adolescents and Teenagers
(Twelve and Older)

The cognitive and psychological phases a child must go through during adolescence present enormous challenges. Experts tell us (as most parents could also) that successfully negotiating the teenage years means balancing who they are with who they want to be with where they come from. The foundation for self-esteem and self-worth has been laid by this time. During these teen years religious, cultural, political, and personal views are explored.

Teens know that death is permanent and universal. They understand the physiological concept of the body and why it stops with death.

Many teens fear being different from their peers. The death of a loved one often upsets this peer status quo. It is important to monitor a bereaved teenager's behavior for several months after a loss. Things to watch out for:

- Attitude change
- Sexual acting out
- Eating habits change
- Alcohol or drug consumption
- Depression and withdrawal

- Dropping out of sports or other activities
- Substantial drop in grades
- Change in music taste
- Unusual cheeriness or hyperactive behavior
- Loss of friends and social life
- Frequent illnesses and missed school
- Inability to discuss deceased
- Weight gain or loss
- Spending much time alone

Adults may notice other grief reactions. If a teen is going through several of these behavioral changes, don't excuse it by saying, "It will get better." Most grief issues need to be discussed and worked through. They never just go away or get better on their own – not even for teenagers.

A Checklist for Dealing
with Grieving Children

1. Don't be shocked if a child doesn't show any common adult grief signs when told of a death loss. Children express their grief quite differently than adults do and sometimes give the impression that they are unaffected by the loss. Children grieve in doses. It is common for children to play, take time out to grieve and then go back to play.

    False joviality, loudness and acting-out are just a few of the behavioral signs to watch for in a bereaved child. Others are: Irritableness, insomnia, sleeping too much, baby-talk, thumb-sucking, or bedwetting. Children may regress "to blankey" or other security symbols that they had given up. Some will cling to a parent and fear separation. Many children ask to leave a light on in their rooms at night (many bereaved adults do too). Often young children will laugh at inappropriate times. This is their way of expressing uneasiness or showing social limitations because of their age.

    Children may want to assume their normal duties (school, play, TV) right after the death of a loved one. These activities may seem inappropriate to an adult, but remember, they are quite normal to a child. Children should be allowed to return to their normal routine as soon as they want.

2. Children will express their grief through play, artwork and even the music they listen to.

Children Express Their Grief in Many Creative Ways

- Pay special attention to any artwork a bereaved child does after the death. Often children will draw their perception of the death, the funeral, and whatever else might be on their minds.

- Be aware of any role-playing the bereaved child may perform with dolls, soldiers, or stuffed animals. Often children make up magical friends to talk with about the death. Story-telling is a way young children can communicate their feelings about a loss.

- In an older child, listen to the type of music he is listening to. Has it changed since the loss? Is it depressing? Does it have death themes?

- Be aware that young and older children who lose a sibling or parent often have thoughts of suicide.

Younger children often want to join their brother or sister or parent who has just died. Together, this seems like a logical thing to do.

3. All children will need to do grief work, just as adults do. Not all children will need therapy or support groups, but many will. There are different schools of thought on how soon a bereaved child should receive therapy, so speaking with an expert (in thanatology) is advisable.
Call your local mental health agency or the Association of Death Educators and Counselors to find out if there are support groups or grief therapists that specialize in childhood grief.

4. Children who have lost a loved one to a terminal illness may start feeling sick and complain about symptoms similar to those the deceased had before he died. (This happens to adults, too.)

5. Children who lose a parent often have difficulty as they approach the age the parent was when he or she died. Some studies show that people who believe they will die at a certain age because a parent did often, indeed, die at that age.

6. Children and teens who have dabbled in drugs or alcohol prior to their loss need to be closely watched when

bereaved. Substance abuse (for many adults as well) often is the "treatment" of choice when dealing with grief.[1]

7. Like adults, children will repeat questions about the loss. Often it becomes annoying to adults. If your child keeps asking the same question, listen carefully and make sure you are clear about what he is really asking. Try re-phrasing your answer. Often young children are really concerned about themselves. Can this happen to me? Could I get sick like this? Could I be run over by a truck? Will my body stop working, too? Who will die next? Children are trying to find the answers that will work for them in accepting their loss.

8. Many experts identify three important concepts for a child to understand in order to have a mature understanding of what death means. They are:
   1. Death is permanent.
   2. Death means the body stops working.
   3. Death will happen to everyone, someday.
   Just because a child cannot cognitively understand all three concepts doesn't mean that he isn't grieving or in pain.

9. Be aware of any guilt or culpability a child may feel over the death. Often a parent or teacher needs to inquire about these feelings because they are scary and relatively new to young children. Let a child know that such feelings are NORMAL when a person loses someone he loves. A good way to bring up this subject may be to say to the child, "Sometimes we feel responsible when someone we love dies. We never are; it's just the way we feel." In very rare cases, when a child is directly responsible for another's death, individual therapy is strongly recommended.

Children Often Feel Responsible in Some Way for the Death

10. Assess how close the child was to the deceased. The death of a distant aunt may not affect the child as much as the death of a friendly neighbor. Remember, children have special relationships with grandparents. A young child doesn't necessarily understand that because a grandparent is old he needs to die. Be sure to recognize this loss.

11. Children should be allowed to memorialize or commemorate a loved one who dies. For young children this can mean drawing a picture or giving a personal possession to be placed in

the casket with the deceased. Many times young children will ask if they can have the bike or favorite toy of their deceased sibling. Parents often wonder how a child can think of such things at such a time. Remember, it is normal for a child to make such a request. Parents may deal with the request by setting aside a special time to give away personal belongings, or they may give them away immediately. Putting together a scrap book of pictures, poems or stories of the deceased is often a meaningful project for bereaved children.

Family Grief and Children

The main point to understand about
family grief is that everyone in the family
grieves, but not together, not in sync. It is
true the family is grieving over the same
family member, but that is where the
similarity ends. Each member, depending
on age and relationship to the deceased,
will grieve in his own individual way. This
unique feature needs to be respected and
acknowledged. The many problems of
parenting become overwhelming when a
parent is dealing with his or her own grief
over the death of a child.

Certain family members may find it hard
to talk about the deceased, others will
withdraw, and others (especially children)
go on with play and the business of living
– often much to the horror of other family
members. Some parents who lose a child
say they lose interest in their surviving
children. This is temporary, but many
children don't know that. If a child is
harboring any guilt over the death of the
family member, the added parental
rejection may make a fantasy a full-blown
issue for the child. Letting a child know
that you are feeling disinterested in
everything at the moment may help the

child sort out his already very confused feelings.

Different types of death losses create different issues.[2] This is true for children, too. For example, children who lose a sibling to suicide often feel guilty and are afraid to express their feelings. An angry, bereaved parent is often unapproachable and scary to those children. So instead of sharing their fears and guilt, these children may clam up and try to make everything better for the bereaved parent. They try to "fix" the loss and somehow feel responsible for everyone's sadness.

The Way a Loved One Dies May Affect the Grief Process

Parents may keep the bedroom of a deceased sibling just as it was prior to his death for an extended period of time: a quite normal and common thing to do. However, this may become difficult for other family members as time goes on. Good communication is important in helping each other out during the grief process.

Some family members may prefer to put away all pictures of the deceased for a while, and others may prefer to have pictures around. Designating a specific room for pictures may be a workable solution.

Many parents have difficulty with holidays[3] and may forget that other family members are having trouble, too. A Christmas or Chanukah will never be the same for a family who has lost a member, so why not discuss it and find out how everyone is feeling and how they'd like to get through it together? Often starting new traditions is helpful for a bereaved family. Sometimes working through old traditions is good, too. Don't assume because you would just as soon not celebrate anything, the rest of the family feels the same.

A good point to remember here is if you are depressed, you need to keep moving in some way, to take some action, because motivation isn't going to come about by itself. So plan a holiday, even if it seems like you are just acting like a robot (which is probably true). Remember a child who has lost a sibling or parent is never going to have the same holiday, either.

Make family time to discuss feelings and memories of the deceased. Parents say they are surprised to hear of the hidden feelings that emerge when a special time is set aside for this purpose. Many times a family stops using the deceased's name. Use the name of the deceased as much as you need to. Give permission to the rest of the family to use it, also. Set aside a special evening to review pictures or old movies or videos of the deceased. This is a good, healthy way to keep in touch with each other's feelings.

Do not be afraid to seek out local support groups, even if it means going alone. Many bereavement groups have divisions for children and teenagers. It is natural for some bereaved children not be able to open up to a parent or sibling about a loss within the family. Encourage them to seek outside support if you feel this would benefit them in their grief process.

The Classroom and Bereaved Children

Is it important to tell a teacher that a student's family member has died?

It is extremely important that a teacher be told that a child is grieving. It is quite natural to expect a spillover of the grief into the classroom. Telling the facts about the death to a teacher and a class allows everyone the opportunity to support the child.

Many adults change their socializing habits, their jobs and sometimes where they live when they are grieving. Children don't have those same options, and more often than not they go back to the same friends, same school and same routine. The more their school understands the loss, the more supported the child will feel.

It some cases a bereaved child may be transferred into a new school. This adjustment, added to the death loss, is quite a challenge for a young child.

Because our world is rich with multiethnic diversity, many children are bilingual, so it is important to note that when people (including children) grieve, they usually do so in their native language.

Native Language and Ethnic Background also Affect a Child's Grief Process

Teachers should know that a bereaved child will often show grief by acting out, withdrawing, behaving violently, expressing unusual or seemingly inappropriate anger, telling lies; by hyperactivity, irritableness, unusual tiredness, frequent absenteeism, risk-taking, or a disinterest in school.

How does the death of a classmate affect children?

The death of a classmate is often a first-time grief experience for grade school and even high school children. Children do not think about dying unless they have personally been exposed to a death, and even then they don't really believe they themselves could die. So a classmate's death creates an extremely threatening and unsettling feeling for most children.

Bereaved classmates will complain of crying easily, low concentration, lack of interest in school and sports, insomnia, fear of the dark, and a general longing for the deceased to return. Young children may want to stay at home for fear of losing someone there.

For children dealing with difficult home situations, the death of a close friend may cause grief from not only the immediate loss but from hidden family issues with which the child is dealing. A child who expresses an unusual amount of grief over the death of a classmate is often dealing with other loss issues that are not obvious to a teacher.

What suggestions are there for a teacher dealing with the sudden death of a student in an elementary grade?

1. Invite the class to write a letter or draw a picture for the parents of the deceased classmate. Encourage older students to keep a journal of their feelings. This is an extremely helpful exercise for adults as well as children.

Also, helping someone else goes a long way in making the child feel better and gives him the opportunity to learn altruistic and social responsibility.

2. Discuss with the class what to do about the empty desk (if there is one). Allow the children to keep it empty for a period of time or until the end of the school year or remove it or decorate it with artwork. After a few weeks check back with the class about how they are feeling about their decision. They may decide to do something different about the desk as they work through their grief. Be prepared for change.

What to Do About the Empty Desk in the Classroom

Bereaved adults say one of the hardest issues they face is feeling out of control and not having any power to do anything about a death. Bereaved children need to feel that they have some control over their grief feelings. Allowing the class to make decisions about what they can do is very important in giving them some sense of control over the death of their classmate.

3. Allowing children to use clay or paints to express their feelings about the death is great therapy for the children and will offer the teacher insights into

what each child is feeling about the death.

Set Aside Time to Talk About the Deceased

4. Setting aside times to discuss the deceased makes it safe for the children to discuss the death. Encourage them to use the deceased's name. This discussion is not to be confused with a support group that may be needed for bereaved children in the school, which would involve parental permission.

5. Often a note home explaining that a classmate has died will alert parents to possible changes. Teachers should check with the deceased's family about exactly what they would like said regarding the nature of the death. For very young children (nursery school age), parents may be invited to a special meeting to determine how the death will be discussed with the other children.

6. If there is a funeral, the teacher will need to get permission for the class to attend. This should be on a voluntary basis only. Some parents may not allow a child to attend the funeral. Make a special effort to talk with the children who are not allowed to attend, and tell them what went on at the funeral. Do a follow-up discussion

or writing exercise to allow children to express how they felt about attending the funeral. Make sure on the day the class attends the funeral that the children do not have to take a difficult test or compete in sport events.

7. Toward the end of the school year, ask the children if they would like to write a final letter to the parents of the deceased. This could allow the children a closure around their grief and would be greatly appreciated by most bereaved parents. This exercise will also allow the class, as a group, to say good-bye to their classmate one final time.

8. A memorial may be appropriate as part of this closure around the loss. Depending on the age of the children and resources available, a scholarship or an annual school event named after the deceased may be appropriate. Other suggestions:

- A book of poems written by the children given to the bereaved parents at a special ceremony.
- Purchasing a plaque to be hung in the main lobby of the school listing or picturing the deceased children who have attended the school.
- Special dedication or mention in the

school's year book. Many commemorative ideas are appropriate for remembering a classmate.

9. A simple but effective tool when talking with young children is to get your body at eye level with them. Kneel down or sit down with a child, so he does not feel overwhelmed or fearful.

Speak to Children at Their Level

Are programs available to help teachers deal with death in the classroom?

Various grief programs have been designed for the classroom to assist teachers with grieving students. About twenty percent of our schools have incorporated a death and dying course into the curriculum. Also, some independent grief consultants specialize in working with children and grief.

These consultants often are hired to provide crisis intervention when a tragedy strikes a community and/or school. You might contact such organizations as: The Good Grief Program, Judge Baker Guidance Center, 295 Longwood Avenue, Boston, Mass. 02115; 1-617-232-8390. Or: Fernside: A Center for Grieving Children, P.O. Box 8944, Cincinnati, Ohio 45208.

Where can I get more information about death education?

The Association for Death Educators and Counselors (ADEC) is a national organization of professionals who specialize in death education and/or counseling. ADEC offers a national certification for teachers and therapists. It offers a certification process, human resource division, professional standards and ethics committee, and a national task force on the status of death education in grades K-12.

ADEC conducts an annual convention and offers a network of support to professionals interested in starting, continuing, or enhancing new or ongoing death and dying educational programs. It is also the hub of current authors on the subject of death and dying and of grief therapists from around the country.

Contact: ADEC (Association for Death Education and Counseling), 638 Prospect Avenue, Hartford, Connecticut 06105-4298; 1-203-232-4825.

The Funeral and Children[4]

Should children be included in the funeral ritual?

The funeral ritual is our traditional way of saying good-bye to our loved ones. Children need the opportunity (just as adults do) to say this final good-bye. Grief experts tell us that this closure is an important part of the grief process.

Usually parents who allow a child to participate in the funeral of a loved one understand the important (although not enjoyable) lesson they are teaching their child. Children are encouraged to be a part of the funeral arrangements and the actual service. It is important that children learn about their own culture's traditions. Each religion has specific customs and rituals. Children who have been left out of this tradition often express as adults some unfinished grief issues still lingering from a childhood loss.

Many funeral homes today offer videos and slide shows especially for young children. Most of these are well done and offer a positive approach to a rather difficult, but necessary, growing-up experience. Some schools are beginning to offer death education classes to acquaint children with death and dying. The religious significance given to a death ritual is individual to each family.

Helpful suggestions for young funeral-goers:

1. Explain to the children where they are going. Explain vocabulary words associated with a funeral. Remember, young children probably don't know the meaning of many of the words they will hear adults using.

2. Give children the option to view the deceased. Most experts agree that viewing the deceased's body is an extremely important part of the grief process. Young children often use "magical thinking" (thinking that their thoughts caused the death). Be prepared to answer seemingly silly questions. Children will ask if the deceased can feel or hear or sit up. Children may also touch the body and ask why it is hard or feels so cold. Adults need to be prepared to give practical answers to these questions.

3. Talk to the children about your traditions. Explain how things will be done at the funeral and why you chose them to be done that way. Include the children in the funeral

arrangements. Allow them to participate in casket selection and other decisions to help reinforce for them the reality of the death.

4. Talk about feelings and let them know they may experience new emotions. Tell them it is okay to talk about feelings, happy or sad.

5. Be available, but not overly protective, during the experience.

6. Many funeral homes have rooms designed for children. This is important, because as we have mentioned before children will grieve, play, grieve, play. Unlike adults, children find it difficult to maintain a serious, dignified mood for any length of time. Don't be shocked if you see a seven-year-old coloring in one room while his mother is being mourned in the next.

7. How you as an adult feel about funerals strongly influences how your children will feel. Try not to communicate myths or exaggerated fears about death to young children; straightforward, honest feelings are the most helpful.

Should children be allowed to view the deceased?

Some experts tell us that the grief process is significantly longer when the body is not viewed. The first reaction of many parents is to spare a child from seeing a sibling or parent dead. However, for many young children, this experience confirms the death. It also may minimize any "magical thinking" a child might use in order to deny the death.

Preparation for viewing should include briefing a child on the experience. Explaining in simple terms how the body stops working, how it will feel, its temperature can help a child have a healthy first-time viewing experience.

Prepare the Child for Viewing the Deceased

Children fear what they don't know. So preparing a child for a funeral is important and extremely valuable for giving him a solid foundation in dealing with this sad but inevitable event.

Funeral directors have a lot of experience in dealing with children. Ask your funeral director if a video or slide show is available. Ask for books you can read to your child. Many funeral homes have libraries available to the public.

What vocabulary words about death will be helpful in preparing a child for the funeral of a loved one?

Following is a list of some words that may help. (Of course, applicability depends on age.)

ashes	hearse
bereaved	memorialist *(a person who sells monuments)*
casket	
cemetery	monument
coach	obituary
coffin	pallbearer
cremation	suicide
deceased	thanatology *(the study of death)*
embalming	
euthanasia	tombstone
funeral	vault
grave	wake

Should a child be allowed to go to the cemetery?

If part of your death ritual includes the cemetery, then trying to hide that from children only confuses them about what does happen. Be prepared to hear numerous questions about the body and the ground. The concept of the body not working anymore isn't fully understood by very young children, so they may ask what may sound like "silly" questions: "How will Grandpa breathe buried in the ground?" "How will Johnny brush his teeth?" Straightforward answers are always the best.

Religion, Grief and Children

What common reactions from children should adults be aware of when a religious interpretation is used to explain death?

A child who is told his mother or sibling has been called by God to live in heaven may not think a whole lot about a God who takes good people out of his life. When death is explained using God as the "taker," many children become fearful and think of God as "mean." (Many adults find this kind of explanation difficult, so it should not strike us as unusual that children will too.) It is extremely important how we explain death to children. If we give death a religious significance, we must be careful not to frighten children or give them an impression of God we do not intend to make.

Children often confuse heaven as being a "place" where the deceased goes. They do not think in terms of a spirit (unless talking about ghosts), but of body. A little boy who dug up his dead gerbil a month after it died remarked to his father that his gerbil could not be in "pet heaven" because it was still in the back yard.

Many religious death traditions create fear and confusion if they aren't explained to children. A woman who was raised in the Jewish Orthodox faith, in which all mirrors are covered after a death, said she would not look in mirrors for months afterwards because she thought she would see the ghost of the deceased. Actually, the custom was intended to remind the bereaved not to be overly concerned about themselves at this time. Since no one explained the custom to her, she grew up with a fear that may have been avoided if someone had communicated with her about the symbolism.

Young children cannot understand deep philosophical answers to their often deep philosophical questions. We know they are limited by their numerous developmental agendas, so answers need

Keeping Fear and Confusion out of Discussions About Death

to be simple, clear, and honest. Faith is a tremendous help to many adults in time of grief. But for others, there is a temporary aversion to a God who they perceive "took" their loved one away. Children are not much different. To tell a child that God took his brother because he was good and God needed him in heaven can be confusing and scary, especially from a child's point of view. Most children haven't read the Book of Job or developed a philosophy or theology about life and death.

It is not important which religion offers the best explanation to children about death. How parents view death, along with their individual religious philosophy, is how a child will come to view death. A family that not only speaks of God as loving and kind, and is also a loving and kind family, will most likely impress a young child with a positive view of God. A family that acknowledges the many travesties of life as tragic, but doesn't assign blame, teaches children a valuable lesson, that certain things happen though we don't always know why. Families who involve themselves in works for the good of others will be subtly encouraging children to explore their own feelings of right and wrong. Children will build their faith as they learn to trust others. Slowly children will develop relationships with God. Although this process may seem like it doesn't directly answer the many complex questions bereaved children often have, it is a beginning. Offering a positive, loving environment within which to *question* is often the first building block in one's faith.

Terminal Illness and Children

If a parent, relative, or family member is dying of a terminal illness, how should this be explained to a child?

Children need to be informed of any life-threatening illness in the family with as much honesty and clarity about the situation as possible. Children have a sixth sense and usually know when something is wrong. Their active imaginations can create all sorts of havoc, so it is critical that nothing be left to their imaginations regarding the facts about the illness.

Young children may become frightened that they may catch the illness or lose someone else in the family. Many times they will ask rather elaborate questions when in fact they are really trying to find out a few basic facts: Will they die next? Will other loved ones die too?

Informing a child of the seriousness of an illness is quite different from quoting mortality rates for specific diseases. A child may ask flat out if So-and-So is going to die, and only the individual questioned knows how to couch the answer. Children, like adults, should never have all hope about healing taken away. Estimating the brevity of someone's life should be used only as a tool to help a child understand that the illness is serious and (if asked) that death is possible.

Will a child need extra attention during the terminal illness of a family member?

Many children say they feel orphaned when a family member is ill. Whether the patient is a sibling or parent, the household is disrupted and most energies and concerns are directed to the patient. Discussing feelings of abandonment is good because it lets children know that the situation is temporary, although it may not seem that way to them or you.

Realizing how all-consuming a terminal illness can be on family time, it is still important to put aside individual time for surviving children. If the patient is a parent of a young child, it is important to give the child special time with the well parent. Young children who lose a parent often get panicked about losing the well one. Reassurance is critical during this time.

Teachers need to be notified of the situation so when the child brings some of his emotional and psychological issues into his classroom, the teacher will be able to respond in a healthy and productive way.

Should children be allowed to visit a terminally ill family member in the hospital?

Many hospitals today allow children to visit in the hospital, and most will make special arrangements for visitors to terminally ill patients. Part of the grieving process for a family dealing with a terminally ill member begins during the illness. The experts call it anticipatory grief.[5] As children are exposed to the illness and the changing physical appearance of their loved one, they will slowly begin to accept the reality of the illness.

Children will often assume that they are responsible for the illness, as mentioned earlier. Make sure that the reason for the illness is explained using all the available facts. Repeat the reason frequently, as young children need to hear it over and over again.

Losing a family member to an illness is not a comfortable or easy thing for a young child to face. However, it is part of life, and the child who is allowed to feel and question and express his anger about the unfairness of the tragic life events around him often grows up with a deeper understanding about himself and life in general.

Again, children may fear they can "catch" the illness of another family member. Before you take a child to the hospital for a visit, explain the nature of the illness to them. It is important for a child to see the patient in a hospital setting. Again, this helps in accepting the reality of the illness and eventual death.

The Terminally Ill Child

Should a child be told about a terminal illness?

As we mentioned in the section above, giving the child as many facts as possible is helpful in allowing him to come to his own conclusions about his illness. As many experts report, the terminally ill child is quite open and knowledgeable about the severity of his illness. Health care professionals report the problem they find most often is with the parents who are unable to accept the illness and therefore unable to effectively support the child.

Sometimes children will pull away emotionally from parents because they sense the pain the parent is in. It is not unusual for a terminally ill child to develop close friendships with hospital personnel and other patients. These children often talk about how good it is to be able to talk about their fears and feelings with someone. Parents who are unable to talk openly with their child about their feelings are protecting themselves and not their child. Terminally ill children are often exceptionally bright and intuitive and *they know what is going on.*

Terminally ill children need permission to talk about what is happening to them. They need a ritual to "finish business" just as adults do. Children near death will often give away personal possessions to family and hospital staff.

One child who was dying apologized individually to every nurse and doctor for being so difficult. He said he did it so his parents would not hang around his hospital room because he knew how difficult it was for them to watch him die.

Footnotes

1 – (page 22): *Using Grief to Grow: A Primer ~ How You Can Help/How to Get Help;* Hartnett, J.; 1993.
2 – (page 26): *Different Losses Different Issues: What to Expect and How to Help;* Hartnett, J.; 1993.
3 – (page 26): *Death Etiquette for the '90s: What to Do/ What to Say;* Hartnett, J.; 1993.
4 – (page 36): *The Funeral: An Endangered Tradition ~ Making Sense of the Final Farewell;* Hartnett, J.; 1993.
5 – (page 46): Symptomatology and Management of Acute Grief, *American Journal of Psychiatry,* 101, 141-148; Lindemann, E.; 1944

References

Bowlby, J. (1980). Loss, sadness and depression. New York: Basic Books, Inc.

DeSpelder, L.A. & Strickland, A.L. (1987). The last dance. 2nd ed. California: Mansfield Publishing Co.

Fox, S.S. (1985). Good grief: helping groups of children when a friend dies. Massachusetts: The New England Association for the Education of Young Children.

Grollman, A.E., Editor (1967). Explaining death to children. Boston: Beacon Press.

Huntly, T. (1991). Helping children grieve. When someone they love dies. Minneapolis: Augsburg.

Kastenbaum, R.J.(1991). Death, society and human experience. New York: Merrill/Macmillan Publishing Co.

Piaget, J. (1965). The child's conceptions of the world. New Jersey: Littlefield, Adams.

Piaget, J. & Inhelder, B. (1969). The psychology of the child. New York: Basic Books.

Rando, T. (1984). Grief, dying and death. Illinois: Research Press Co.

Raphael, B. (1983). The anatomy of bereavement. New York: Basic Books, Inc.

Rudolph, M. (1978). Should the children know? Encounters with death in the lives of children. New York: Schocken Books.

Wass, H., Berardo, F., Neimeyer, R. (1988). Dying: facing the facts. Washington: Hemisphere Publishing Corp.

Prepare yourself for one of the most difficult jobs you'll ever have: Grief.

If your bookstore or employer does not have the other books in this series, please indicate which ones and how many you need on the form below; cost of each book is $6.95, or $29.95 for the set.

Good Mourning also publishes a set of sympathy note cards (and envelopes) with artwork designed by children who have died. Included is a bookmark with suggested messages of sympathy, to facilitate your own written expression of sympathy to the bereaved – a poignant and personal way to express your sympathy. The cost of a set of 12 note cards/bookmarks is $9.95, plus postage and handling. Please send a check or money order for the total to:

Good Mourning
P.O. 9355
South Burlington, VT 05407-9355

Name of Book	Quantity	Each	Price
Using Grief to Grow: A Primer *How You Can Help/How to Get Help*		$6.95	
Different Losses Different Issues: *What to Expect and How to Help.*		$6.95	
The Funeral: An Endangered Tradition *Making Sense of the Final Farewell*		$6.95	
Grief in the Workplace: *40 Hours Plus Overtime*		$6.95	
Children and Grief: *Big Issues for Little Hearts*		$6.95	
Death Etiquette for the '90s: *What to Do/ What to Say*		$6.95	
Set of Six Books		$29.95	
Note Cards (one dozen, plus envelopes)		$9.95	
Subtotal			
Tax, if applicable			
Shipping/handling ($2.25 ea/$8 set)			
Total (check enclosed)			

Phone: 802-658-5883

Ship to:

*Name*_____

*Address*_____

*City*_____*State*_____*ZIP*_____

If you would like to submit a question regarding the death of a loved one, or learn how to support a friend who has lost a loved one, please do so in the space below or on your paper. I will be happy to respond to as many questions as I can.

With warmest regards, Johnette Hartnett

_____

_____

_____

_____

_____

_____

_____

_____

_____

_____

_____

_____

_____

_____

_____

_____

_____

_____

_____

_____

_____

_____

_____

_____

_____

_____

_____

_____